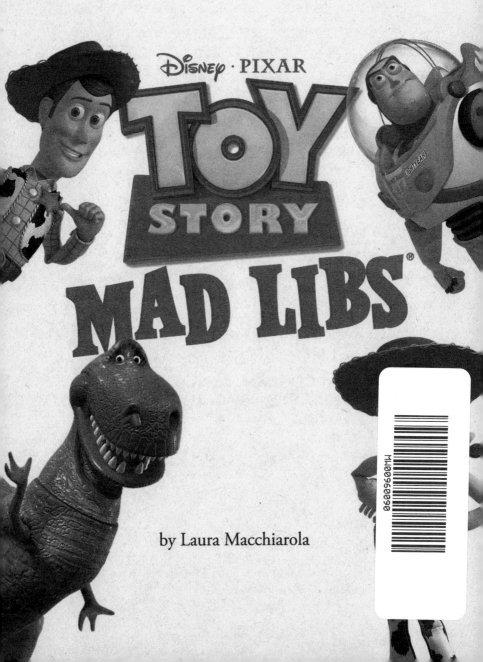

Disney · PIXAR

TOY STORY
MAD LIBS

by Laura Macchiarola

MAD LIBS
An Imprint of Penguin Random House LLC, New York

Mad Libs format copyright © 2019 by Penguin Random House LLC. All rights reserved.

Concept created by Roger Price & Leonard Stern

Copyright © 2019 Disney Enterprises, Inc. and Pixar

Published by Mad Libs,
an imprint of Penguin Random House LLC, New York.
Printed in the USA.

Visit us online at www.penguinrandomhouse.com.

ISBN 9781524792008
1 3 5 7 9 10 8 6 4 2

MAD LIBS

INSTRUCTIONS

MAD LIBS® is a game for people who don't like games!
It can be played by one, two, three, four, or forty.

● RIDICULOUSLY SIMPLE DIRECTIONS

In this tablet you will find stories containing blank spaces where words
are left out. One player, the READER, selects one of these stories. The
READER does not tell anyone what the story is about. Instead, he/she asks
the other players, the WRITERS, to give him/her words. These words are
used to fill in the blank spaces in the story.

● TO PLAY

The READER asks each WRITER in turn to call out a word—an adjective or
a noun or whatever the space calls for—and uses them to fill in the blank
spaces in the story. The result is a MAD LIBS® game.

When the READER then reads the completed MAD LIBS® game to the other
players, they will discover that they have written a story that is fantastic,
screamingly funny, shocking, silly, crazy, or just plain dumb—depending
upon which words each WRITER called out.

● EXAMPLE (*Before* and *After*)

" _____ !" he said _____
      EXCLAMATION   ADVERB

as he jumped into his convertible _____ and
                                         NOUN

drove off with his _____ wife.
                     ADJECTIVE

" _____ **OUCH** _____ !" he said _____ **STUPIDLY** _____
      EXCLAMATION   ADVERB

as he jumped into his convertible _____ **CAT** _____ and
                                         NOUN

drove off with his _____ **BRAVE** _____ wife.
                     ADJECTIVE

In case you have forgotten what adjectives, adverbs, nouns, and verbs are, here is a quick review:

An ADJECTIVE describes something or somebody. *Lumpy, soft, ugly, messy,* and *short* are adjectives.

An ADVERB tells how something is done. It modifies a verb and usually ends in "ly." *Modestly, stupidly, greedily,* and *carefully* are adverbs.

A NOUN is the name of a person, place, or thing. *Sidewalk, umbrella, bridle, bathtub,* and *nose* are nouns.

A VERB is an action word. *Run, pitch, jump,* and *swim* are verbs. Put the verbs in past tense if the directions say PAST TENSE. *Ran, pitched, jumped,* and *swam* are verbs in the past tense.

When we ask for A PLACE, we mean any sort of place: a country or city (*Spain, Cleveland*) or a room (*bathroom, kitchen*).

An EXCLAMATION or SILLY WORD is any sort of funny sound, gasp, grunt, or outcry, like *Wow!, Ouch!, Whomp!, Ick!,* and *Gadzooks!*

When we ask for specific words, like a NUMBER, a COLOR, an ANIMAL, or a PART OF THE BODY, we mean a word that is one of those things, like *seven, blue, horse,* or *head.*

When we ask for a PLURAL, it means more than one. For example, *cat* pluralized is *cats.*

MAD LIBS® is fun to play with friends, but you can also play it by yourself! To begin with, DO NOT look at the story on the page below. Fill in the blanks on this page with the words called for. Then, using the words you have selected, fill in the blank spaces in the story.

Now you've created your own hilarious MAD LIBS® game!

GOOD MORNING, TOYS

A PLACE _McDonalds_

PLURAL NOUN _shoes_

ADJECTIVE _love_

TYPE OF FOOD _pizza_

ADJECTIVE _kind_

ADJECTIVE _mean_

ANIMAL (PLURAL) _cats_

PART OF THE BODY _butt_

NUMBER _125_

PLURAL NOUN _cooke_

ADJECTIVE _nice_

ADJECTIVE _pretty_

TYPE OF FOOD _sushi_

TYPE OF FOOD (PLURAL) _cookies_

NOUN _pen_

MAD LIBS

GOOD MORNING, TOYS

It's just another day in Andy's _____. Let's see what the

A PLACE

_____ are doing on this _____ morning.

PLURAL NOUN ADJECTIVE

Mr. _____ Head: Ha! Now that I've stolen Bo Peep's sheep,

TYPE OF FOOD

I'll make a fortune selling their rare, _____ fleece.

ADJECTIVE

Bo Peep: Stop it, you mean, _____ potato! Won't somebody

ADJECTIVE

help my poor _____?

ANIMAL (PLURAL)

Woody: Is Mr. Potato _____ . . . uh, I mean _____-Eyed

PART OF THE BODY NUMBER

Bart giving you a hard time, Bo Peep? I'm getting real tired of your

_____, One-Eyed Bart!

PLURAL NOUN

Mr. Potato Head: What are you going to do about it, Sheriff? I brought

my _____ attack dog, Slinky!

ADJECTIVE

Woody: Well, I brought my dinosaur, Rex, who eats _____ dogs!

ADJECTIVE

Mr. Potato Head: Not so fast, Sheriff! Does anyone else smell

_____?

TYPE OF FOOD

Mom: Andy! Time for dinner! We're having your favorite:

_____!

TYPE OF FOOD (PLURAL)

Andy: All right, Mom! Be down in a/an _____!

NOUN

MAD LIBS® is fun to play with friends, but you can also play it by yourself! To begin with, DO NOT look at the story on the page below. Fill in the blanks on this page with the words called for. Then, using the words you have selected, fill in the blank spaces in the story.

Now you've created your own hilarious MAD LIBS® game!

MEET THE TOYS, PART 1

PLURAL NOUN _____

A PLACE _____

NOUN _____

ARTICLE OF CLOTHING (PLURAL) _____

NOUN _____

ADJECTIVE _____

PLURAL NOUN _____

ARTICLE OF CLOTHING _____

NOUN _____

ADJECTIVE _____

ANIMAL _____

PART OF THE BODY (PLURAL) _____

NUMBER _____

SILLY WORD _____

MAD LIBS

MEET THE TOYS, PART 1

Would you like to get to know the _____ in Andy's room?
PLURAL NOUN

Let's meet some of the gang:

Woody: The sheriff in (the) _____, and Andy's favorite
A PLACE

_____! He's brave, loyal, and looks great in cowboy
NOUN

_____.
ARTICLE OF CLOTHING (PLURAL)

Buzz _____-year: The coolest toy ever, and Woody's most
NOUN

_____ friend! He can fly, talk, and shoot _____
ADJECTIVE   PLURAL NOUN

out of his _____!
ARTICLE OF CLOTHING

Mr. Potato Head: The best-dressed _____ in Andy's room.
NOUN

He's got a bit of an attitude—watch out for his _____ eyes!
ADJECTIVE

Rex: This guy is more of a scaredy-_____ than a dinosaur. He
ANIMAL

might have short _____, but at least he has a big
PART OF THE BODY (PLURAL)

heart.

Hamm: This piggy bank holds over _____ dollars in change!
NUMBER

Challenge him to a game of _____ if you're feeling lucky.
SILLY WORD

MAD LIBS® is fun to play with friends, but you can also play it by yourself! To begin with, DO NOT look at the story on the page below. Fill in the blanks on this page with the words called for. Then, using the words you have selected, fill in the blank spaces in the story.

Now you've created your own hilarious MAD LIBS® game!

WOODY'S STAFF MEETING

NUMBER _____

EXCLAMATION _____

NOUN _____

PLURAL NOUN _____

PLURAL NOUN _____

NOUN _____

NOUN _____

PART OF THE BODY _____

PERSON IN ROOM _____

NOUN _____

ADJECTIVE _____

VERB ENDING IN "ING" _____

TYPE OF FOOD _____

PLURAL NOUN _____

NOUN _____

NOUN _____

MAD LIBS®

WOODY'S STAFF MEETING

Hello? Mic check: 1 . . . 2 . . . _____ . Can everybody hear me?
<u>NUMBER</u>

_____! Thank you all for attending today's _____
<u>EXCLAMATION</u>   <u>NOUN</u>

meeting. We've got a lot of _____ to cover, so let's get
<u>PLURAL NOUN</u>

started! First, moving day is only seven _____ away, and I
<u>PLURAL NOUN</u>

don't want any _____ left behind during the move. Make sure
<u>NOUN</u>

you've got a moving _____! Next, Mr. Potato _____ is
<u>NOUN</u>   <u>PART OF THE BODY</u>

going to lead a seminar called "Playtime with Style" this week. If you're

interested in attending, please sign up with _____. Slinky
<u>PERSON IN ROOM</u>

will also host a/an _____ on how to untangle yourself after a/an
<u>NOUN</u>

_____ playtime. I highly recommend _____ that
<u>ADJECTIVE</u>   <u>VERB ENDING IN "ING"</u>

one if you have trouble with that sort of thing. Finally, I wanted to

remind you all that _____ Planet prizes are _____
<u>TYPE OF FOOD</u>   <u>PLURAL NOUN</u>

just like the rest of us. Whenever Andy brings one home, be courteous

and give that toy a big _____! Well, that was everything on
<u>NOUN</u>

my _____. Toys dismissed!
<u>NOUN</u>

MAD LIBS® is fun to play with friends, but you can also play it by yourself! To begin with, DO NOT look at the story on the page below. Fill in the blanks on this page with the words called for. Then, using the words you have selected, fill in the blank spaces in the story.

Now you've created your own hilarious MAD LIBS® game!

SARGE LEADS THE TROOPS

EXCLAMATION _____

PERSON IN ROOM _____

NOUN _____

VERB _____

NOUN _____

PART OF THE BODY _____

SILLY WORD _____

ANIMAL _____

NOUN _____

PLURAL NOUN _____

ADJECTIVE _____

TYPE OF FOOD _____

NOUN _____

PLURAL NOUN _____

MAD LIBS

SARGE LEADS THE TROOPS

_____, troops—look alive! Our mission is to infiltrate
　　EXCLAMATION

_____'s birthday party and find out what's inside those
PERSON IN ROOM

presents. Failure is not a/an _____—the toys of Andy's room
　　　　　　　　　　　　　NOUN

are counting on us—so let's move, move, _____!
　　　　　　　　　　　　　　　VERB

- First and foremost, a good soldier never leaves a/an _____

  behind! If your comrade takes a fall, take a moment to lend a

  helping _____.
  　　PART OF THE BODY

- Secondly, teamwork is everything! We need to work together to

  carry Andy's walkie-_____ downstairs and transmit audio
  　　　　　　　SILLY WORD

  back to our general, Woody. Remember: His code name is Mother

  _____.
  　ANIMAL

- Finally, report each and every _____ that is unwrapped.
  　　　　　　　　　　　　　NOUN

  Whether it's a lunch box, blanket, or _____, we must
  　　　　　　　　　　　　　PLURAL NOUN

  be diligent and _____ in our duties!
  　　　　　ADJECTIVE

We will not rest until every gift is opened, every slice of _____
　　　　　　　　　　　　　　　　　　　　　　TYPE OF FOOD

is eaten, and every _____ comes down from his or her sugar
　　　　　　　NOUN

rush. Stick to your training, and best of luck, _____!
　　　　　　　　　　　　　　　　　PLURAL NOUN

MAD LIBS® is fun to play with friends, but you can also play it by yourself! To begin with, DO NOT look at the story on the page below. Fill in the blanks on this page with the words called for. Then, using the words you have selected, fill in the blank spaces in the story.

Now you've created your own hilarious MAD LIBS® game!

BUZZ LIGHTYEAR TO THE RESCUE!

VERB _____

SAME VERB _____

EXCLAMATION _____

ADJECTIVE _____

PLURAL NOUN _____

SILLY WORD _____

NOUN _____

OCCUPATION _____

A PLACE _____

NOUN _____

PART OF THE BODY _____

NOUN _____

A PLACE _____

MAD LIBS®
BUZZ LIGHTYEAR
TO THE RESCUE!

Buzz Lightyear to Star Command—do you _____? Star
_____VERB

Command, do you _____? _____, why don't
_____SAME VERB____EXCLAMATION

they answer?!

Mission log: I've just awakened from years of _____-sleep to
_____ADJECTIVE

find myself surrounded by _____! They're probably minions
_____PLURAL NOUN

of _____. I've tried in vain to contact Star Command, but no
___SILLY WORD

one's responded to my _____. Now I must rely on my skills as
_____NOUN

a/an _____ to navigate my way back to (the) _____.
_____OCCUPATION_____A PLACE

Even now, Zurg is likely preparing a/an _____ that could
_____NOUN

destroy the entire galaxy. Since I alone know his only weakness—his

Achilles' _____—I can't delay any longer! The _____
_____PART OF THE BODY_____NOUN

is counting on me . . . to (the) _____ and beyond!
_____A PLACE

MAD LIBS® is fun to play with friends, but you can also play it by yourself! To begin with, DO NOT look at the story on the page below. Fill in the blanks on this page with the words called for. Then, using the words you have selected, fill in the blank spaces in the story.

Now you've created your own hilarious MAD LIBS® game!

YOU ARE A TOY!

NOUN _____

NOUN _____

ADJECTIVE _____

ARTICLE OF CLOTHING (PLURAL) _____

EXCLAMATION _____

ADJECTIVE _____

OCCUPATION _____

ADJECTIVE _____

ADVERB _____

ADJECTIVE _____

PART OF THE BODY _____

PLURAL NOUN _____

NOUN _____

PLURAL NOUN _____

A PLACE _____

VERB _____

MAD LIBS®

YOU ARE A TOY!

When Buzz's spaceship first crash-landed on Andy's _____,
                                                        NOUN

Woody didn't take too kindly to the new _____ in town. He
                                                NOUN

thought Andy's room was only _____ enough for one favorite
                                    ADJECTIVE

toy. While Buzz charmed the _____ off of
                                ARTICLE OF CLOTHING (PLURAL)

Andy's other toys, Woody wanted to say "_____" right in
                                              EXCLAMATION

Buzz Lightyear's _____ face. Furthermore, Buzz believed that
                      ADJECTIVE

he was a *real* _____ and not a toy at all! Woody called him
                  OCCUPATION

delusional and _____, but Buzz didn't care. It wasn't until
                    ADJECTIVE

Woody _____ knocked Buzz out of Andy's window that
          ADVERB

things *really* started to get _____. The two toys went
                                    ADJECTIVE

toe-to-_____ until they realized they were lost. Finally, Woody
          PART OF THE BODY

and Buzz set their _____ aside and worked together to find
                        PLURAL NOUN

their way back _____. In the end, the two became the best
                    NOUN

of _____, and even as Andy grows up and goes to
        PLURAL NOUN

(the) _____, their friendship will continue to _____!
          A PLACE   VERB

MAD LIBS® is fun to play with friends, but you can also play it by yourself! To begin with, DO NOT look at the story on the page below. Fill in the blanks on this page with the words called for. Then, using the words you have selected, fill in the blank spaces in the story.

Now you've created your own hilarious MAD LIBS® game!

HAMM IT UP

PLURAL NOUN _____

VERB ENDING IN "ING" _____

ADJECTIVE _____

VERB ENDING IN "ING" _____

VERB _____

NOUN _____

NOUN _____

PLURAL NOUN _____

ANIMAL (PLURAL) _____

PLURAL NOUN _____

ARTICLE OF CLOTHING _____

PART OF THE BODY _____

NOUN _____

VERB ENDING IN "ING" _____

MAD LIBS

HAMM IT UP

Listen, if you want to make it in Andy's room, there are a few

_____ that you've gotta understand. Let's start with the basics:
PLURAL NOUN

- **DON'T** let Andy or Mom catch you talking or _____!
  VERB ENDING IN "ING"

  Remember, this is all a/an _____ secret. When you hear
  ADJECTIVE

  somebody shout "Andy's _____," get back to your
  VERB ENDING IN "ING"

  position and _____!
  VERB

- **DO** let loose and have fun when it's playtime! Nobody likes

  a/an _____ in the mud. If Andy wants you to be the hero
  NOUN

  or the _____, just go with it.
  NOUN

- **DON'T** let Rex get on your _____. Sure, he might be
  PLURAL NOUN

  annoying, but that's _____ for you.
  ANIMAL (PLURAL)

- **DO** play _____ with Mr. Potato Head if he wants to
  PLURAL NOUN

  gamble. You might get a sweet _____ or a/an
  ARTICLE OF CLOTHING

  _____ if you win!
  PART OF THE BODY

In short, be a good _____ to Andy, don't get caught
NOUN

_____, yada yada yada. Have fun!
VERB ENDING IN "ING"

MAD LIBS® is fun to play with friends, but you can also play it by yourself! To begin with, DO NOT look at the story on the page below. Fill in the blanks on this page with the words called for. Then, using the words you have selected, fill in the blank spaces in the story.

Now you've created your own hilarious MAD LIBS® game!

COWBOY CATCHPHRASES

EXCLAMATION _____

VERB ENDING IN "ING" _____

NOUN _____

NOUN _____

ANIMAL _____

NOUN _____

ADJECTIVE _____

SILLY WORD _____

NOUN _____

NOUN _____

ADJECTIVE _____

ADJECTIVE _____

ADJECTIVE _____

ANIMAL (PLURAL) _____

COWBOY CATCHPHRASES

_____, partner! If you're lookin' for a rootin'-_____

EXCLAMATION   VERB ENDING IN "ING"

time, just pull on Sheriff Woody's _____ and have a listen:

NOUN

- "Reach for the _____!"

NOUN

- "There's a/an _____ in my boot!"

ANIMAL

- "Somebody's poisoned the _____!"

NOUN

- "This town ain't _____ enough for the two of us!"

ADJECTIVE

- "Yee-haw! Giddyup, _____!"

SILLY WORD

- "You're my favorite _____!"

NOUN

- "I'd like to join your _____, boys, but first, I'm gonna

NOUN

  sing a/an _____ song."

ADJECTIVE

No other cowboy doll is as friendly or _____ as Woody! With

ADJECTIVE

the sheriff on your side, you'll be havin' _____ West adventures

ADJECTIVE

till the _____ come home.

ANIMAL (PLURAL)

MAD LIBS® is fun to play with friends, but you can also play it by yourself! To begin with, DO NOT look at the story on the page below. Fill in the blanks on this page with the words called for. Then, using the words you have selected, fill in the blank spaces in the story.

Now you've created your own hilarious MAD LIBS® game!

PIZZA PLANET

ADJECTIVE _____

NOUN _____

TYPE OF FOOD _____

ADJECTIVE _____

COLOR _____

PART OF THE BODY _____

NUMBER _____

NOUN _____

TYPE OF FOOD (PLURAL) _____

NOUN _____

NUMBER _____

OCCUPATION _____

MAD LIBS

PIZZA PLANET

Welcome, space traveler, to Pizza Planet—the most _____

ADJECTIVE

pizzeria in the galaxy! Once you land your _____, refuel with

NOUN

some pepperoni and _____. Then, make your way to the

TYPE OF FOOD

arcade for a/an _____ Alien encounter! You'll come across

ADJECTIVE

thousands of _____ Aliens piled up as far as the _____

COLOR   PART OF THE BODY

can see, but "the Claw" will only allow you to choose _____.

NUMBER

Afterward, refresh yourself with a big _____ of Alien vomit—

NOUN

great for washing down an order of _____! Before

TYPE OF FOOD (PLURAL)

you blast off back to your home _____, stop by the air hockey

NOUN

table for some one-on- _____ action. Defend your high score as

NUMBER

any good space _____ would!

OCCUPATION

MAD LIBS® is fun to play with friends, but you can also play it by yourself! To begin with, DO NOT look at the story on the page below. Fill in the blanks on this page with the words called for. Then, using the words you have selected, fill in the blank spaces in the story.

Now you've created your own hilarious MAD LIBS® game!

WOODY'S GUIDE TO SURVIVING SID'S ROOM

ADJECTIVE _____

ADJECTIVE _____

VERB _____

PLURAL NOUN _____

ANIMAL _____

ADJECTIVE _____

PLURAL NOUN _____

VERB _____

PART OF THE BODY (PLURAL) _____

ANIMAL _____

NOUN _____

TYPE OF FOOD _____

PART OF THE BODY _____

PLURAL NOUN _____

CELEBRITY _____

MAD LIBS
WOODY'S GUIDE TO
SURVIVING SID'S ROOM

Listen up, partner! I've got some _____ advice if you're ever
<u>ADJECTIVE</u>

_____ enough to end up in Sid's room. As Buzz once said,
<u>ADJECTIVE</u>

"Whatever you do, don't _____." Just stay calm, and follow
<u>VERB</u>

these _____:
<u>PLURAL NOUN</u>

1. Watch out for Scud the _____! He's just as _____
   <u>ANIMAL</u>   <u>ADJECTIVE</u>

   as his owner and has a habit of chewing up poor, defenseless

   _____. If you hear barking, just _____!
   <u>PLURAL NOUN</u>   <u>VERB</u>

2. Make friends! Toys like Babyface, _____,
   <u>PART OF THE BODY (PLURAL)</u>

   and the _____ will help you make it through the night.
   <u>ANIMAL</u>

   Without them, I could never have staged a/an _____ to
   <u>NOUN</u>

   rescue Buzz!

3. Sid likes to leave half-eaten bowls of _____ around—use
   <u>TYPE OF FOOD</u>

   them to your advantage! A splash of milk on your _____
   <u>PART OF THE BODY</u>

   will keep you alert and heal any _____ on your plastic
   <u>PLURAL NOUN</u>

   face.

4. Don't lose hope! If _____ and I can make it out of Sid's
   <u>CELEBRITY</u>

   room alive, so can you!

MAD LIBS® is fun to play with friends, but you can also play it by yourself! To begin with, DO NOT look at the story on the page below. Fill in the blanks on this page with the words called for. Then, using the words you have selected, fill in the blank spaces in the story.

Now you've created your own hilarious MAD LIBS® game!

SLINKY SPEAKS

NOUN _____

ADJECTIVE _____

ANIMAL _____

PLURAL NOUN _____

PART OF THE BODY (PLURAL) _____

ANIMAL _____

A PLACE _____

VERB ENDING IN "ING" _____

ANIMAL (PLURAL) _____

ADJECTIVE _____

ANIMAL _____

SILLY WORD _____

ANIMAL _____

NOUN _____

MAD LIBS

SLINKY SPEAKS

Even though I'm a slinky _____, I've always felt as loyal and
                                   NOUN

as _____ as a real four-legged friend. Being the only family
    ADJECTIVE

_____ was really nice for a while. Playtime was full of
     ANIMAL

_____ and scratches behind the _____.
  PLURAL NOUN   PART OF THE BODY (PLURAL)

That is, until one Christmas, when a *real* _____ named
                                         ANIMAL

Buster joined the family! Who would have thought having a puppy in

(the) _____ would be so great? Buster would run up to us
     A PLACE

toys, barking and _____, and he'd play with us till the
         VERB ENDING IN "ING"

_____ came home. He helped us rescue toys from Mom's
 ANIMAL (PLURAL)

_____ yard sales, such as Wheezy the squeaky _____.
  ADJECTIVE   ANIMAL

And *finally*, I have someone to speak "dog" to—not even my best pal,

Woody, understands me when I say "woof" or "_____!"
                                     SILLY WORD

Buster's puppy years are long gone, but from one _____ to
                                     ANIMAL

another, he's still a very good _____!
                      NOUN

MAD LIBS® is fun to play with friends, but you can also play it by yourself! To begin with, DO NOT look at the story on the page below. Fill in the blanks on this page with the words called for. Then, using the words you have selected, fill in the blank spaces in the story.

Now you've created your own hilarious MAD LIBS® game!

WOODY'S ROUNDUP

NOUN _____

TYPE OF FOOD _____

OCCUPATION _____

ANIMAL _____

ADJECTIVE _____

ANIMAL _____

A PLACE _____

ADJECTIVE _____

NOUN _____

NOUN _____

ADJECTIVE _____

ADJECTIVE _____

PLURAL NOUN _____

ADJECTIVE _____

MAD LIBS

WOODY'S ROUNDUP

Tune in to *Woody's Roundup*, brought to you by _____
NOUN

Crunchies, the crunchiest _____ there is! Join Woody and his
TYPE OF FOOD

whole posse, including Jessie the yodelin' _____! She sings
OCCUPATION

like a/an _____, and can even speak to _____
ANIMAL ADJECTIVE

critters. You'll also meet Bullseye, Woody's _____—
ANIMAL

the smartest steed in (the) _____. There's also the
A PLACE

_____ Prospector, Stinky Pete, a bumbling _____
ADJECTIVE NOUN

who can never seem to remember where he left his _____.
NOUN

Last, but certainly not _____, there's Sheriff Woody—the
ADJECTIVE

rootin'-est tootin'-est cowboy in the wild, _____ West!
ADJECTIVE

This week on *Woody's Roundup*, find out if Woody and Bullseye save

the local _____ before _____ Pete's dynamite goes
PLURAL NOUN ADJECTIVE

off! Don't miss it, partner!

MAD LIBS® is fun to play with friends, but you can also play it by yourself! To begin with, DO NOT look at the story on the page below. Fill in the blanks on this page with the words called for. Then, using the words you have selected, fill in the blank spaces in the story.

Now you've created your own hilarious MAD LIBS® game!

MEET THE TOYS, PART 2

PERSON IN ROOM _____

EXCLAMATION _____

PLURAL NOUN _____

TYPE OF FOOD _____

ADJECTIVE _____

PART OF THE BODY (PLURAL) _____

ADJECTIVE _____

PART OF THE BODY _____

NOUN _____

VERB ENDING IN "ING" _____

NOUN _____

NOUN _____

ADJECTIVE _____

CELEBRITY _____

PLURAL NOUN _____

TYPE OF FOOD _____

NOUN _____

MAD LIBS®

MEET THE TOYS, PART 2

You've already met some of the toys in _____'s room. Say
PERSON IN ROOM

"_____" to a brand-new group of _____:
EXCLAMATION   PLURAL NOUN

Slinky Dog: A genteel Southern canine who looks like a/an

_____! He's also the most _____ dog you'll ever lay
TYPE OF FOOD   ADJECTIVE

_____ on.
PART OF THE BODY (PLURAL)

Bo Peep: This _____ doll must watch over her sheep and
ADJECTIVE

keep a/an _____ out for One-Eyed Bart! Rumor has it
PART OF THE BODY

that she and Woody are a/an _____.
NOUN

Jessie: The _____ cowgirl with a song in her heart and
VERB ENDING IN "ING"

a/an _____ in her step. You'll often find her with her best
NOUN

_____, Bullseye!
NOUN

Wheezy: A squeaky, _____ penguin with a *big* singing voice!
ADJECTIVE

For such a little guy, he sings just like _____!
CELEBRITY

The LGMs: That stands for Little Green _____! These
PLURAL NOUN

dudes are from _____ Planet, and their deity is known as "the
TYPE OF FOOD

_____."
NOUN

MAD LIBS® is fun to play with friends, but you can also play it by yourself! To begin with, DO NOT look at the story on the page below. Fill in the blanks on this page with the words called for. Then, using the words you have selected, fill in the blank spaces in the story.

Now you've created your own hilarious MAD LIBS® game!

BUZZ'S ESCAPE PLAN

PLURAL NOUN _____

A PLACE _____

TYPE OF FOOD _____

PLURAL NOUN _____

VERB _____

NOUN _____

ADJECTIVE _____

ADJECTIVE _____

PLURAL NOUN _____

NOUN _____

ADJECTIVE _____

NOUN _____

PART OF THE BODY _____

MAD LIBS®

BUZZ'S ESCAPE PLAN

All right, _____, here's the plan for breaking out of
PLURAL NOUN

(the) _____:
A PLACE

- Mr. and Mrs. _____ Head: You distract Mom by leaving
  TYPE OF FOOD

  your _____ all over the floor.
  PLURAL NOUN

- While she's putting you back together, Jessie will _____
  VERB

  for Buster and ride down the _____ until they're out the
  NOUN

  front door. Jessie, this part is perfect for you, since your riding skills

  are so _____. But if you have a/an _____ idea,
  ADJECTIVE   ADJECTIVE

  just let me know.

- Ahem, where was I? Ah yes—Slinky, you'll carry Woody and me

  down the _____ while Jessie rings the _____
  PLURAL NOUN   NOUN

  from outside. This will create a/an _____ cover while
  ADJECTIVE

  Mom goes to answer the _____.
  NOUN

- Once we're all finally outside, that just leaves Rex. Rex, your role

  here is to use your _____!
  PART OF THE BODY

MAD LIBS® is fun to play with friends, but you can also play it by yourself! To begin with, DO NOT look at the story on the page below. Fill in the blanks on this page with the words called for. Then, using the words you have selected, fill in the blank spaces in the story.

Now you've created your own hilarious MAD LIBS® game!

THE ROUGHEST, TOUGHEST COWGIRL

OCCUPATION _____

ANIMAL _____

COLOR _____

PART OF THE BODY _____

ANIMAL (PLURAL) _____

ADJECTIVE _____

NOUN _____

NOUN _____

VERB ENDING IN "ING" _____

NOUN _____

ADJECTIVE _____

NOUN _____

MAD LIBS
THE ROUGHEST,
TOUGHEST COWGIRL

Yee-haw! Life as a yodelin' _____ sure is peachy in Andy's
                                OCCUPATION

room. First off, there's a ton of critters running around, such

as Bullseye the _____, Buster the dog, Hamm the pig, and
                    ANIMAL

those little _____ Aliens that won't stop following Mr. Potato
                COLOR

_____ everywhere. I miss the rabbits, squirrels,
    PART OF THE BODY

and _____ of the prairie, but these new critters are
        ANIMAL (PLURAL)

_____ helpful! Second, a rodeo ain't nothin' compared to the
  ADJECTIVE

_____ in Andy's room! If you take one of the race cars for
  NOUN

a/an _____, you'll be hootin' and _____ in
        NOUN   VERB ENDING IN "ING"

no time flat. Third, even if Mom packs you away in a/an _____,
                                                            NOUN

you'll always have good friends to keep you _____. Buzz is
                                                ADJECTIVE

always there for me—he's not half bad for a space-_____!
                                                        NOUN

MAD LIBS® is fun to play with friends, but you can also play it by yourself! To begin with, DO NOT look at the story on the page below. Fill in the blanks on this page with the words called for. Then, using the words you have selected, fill in the blank spaces in the story.

Now you've created your own hilarious MAD LIBS® game!

SPACE RANGER OR SPACE TOY?

VERB _____

ADJECTIVE _____

ADJECTIVE _____

ARTICLE OF CLOTHING _____

ADJECTIVE _____

OCCUPATION _____

NOUN _____

ADJECTIVE _____

SILLY WORD _____

NOUN _____

PLURAL NOUN _____

NOUN _____

VERB _____

PART OF THE BODY (PLURAL) _____

NOUN _____

MAD LIBS
SPACE RANGER
OR SPACE TOY?

As Buzz's best friend, I've had to _____ with a few different

VERB

Buzz _____-years in my time. Here's how to know if you're

ADJECTIVE

dealing with the real Buzz *or* with a/an "_____" space ranger:

ADJECTIVE

1. Does your Buzz wear a/an _____ over his head?

ARTICLE OF CLOTHING

    If the answer is "yes," that means he thinks the air is _____.

ADJECTIVE

    Your Buzz believes he's a space ranger!

2. Does your Buzz blush around a certain red-haired _____?

OCCUPATION

    You've got yourself the real Buzz Light-_____.

NOUN

3. Does your Buzz talk nonstop about defeating the _____

ADJECTIVE

    emperor, _____? If so, you've got yourself a/an

SILLY WORD

    _____ ranger, pal.

NOUN

4. Does your Buzz create elaborate schemes with everyday

    _____, such as traffic cones, a mop, or a/an _____?

PLURAL NOUN   NOUN

    That's definitely the real Buzz.

If you're dealing with a "real" space ranger, don't _____! Get

VERB

your _____ on a genuine Buzz Lightyear manual

PART OF THE BODY (PLURAL)

and hit the reset _____!

NOUN

MAD LIBS® is fun to play with friends, but you can also play it by yourself! To begin with, DO NOT look at the story on the page below. Fill in the blanks on this page with the words called for. Then, using the words you have selected, fill in the blank spaces in the story.

Now you've created your own hilarious MAD LIBS® game!

OVER THIRTY ACCESSORIES

SILLY WORD _____

PART OF THE BODY _____

PLURAL NOUN _____

EXCLAMATION _____

ADJECTIVE _____

TYPE OF FOOD (PLURAL) _____

PART OF THE BODY (PLURAL) _____

PLURAL NOUN _____

VERB ENDING IN "ING" _____

NOUN _____

PART OF THE BODY (PLURAL) _____

ANIMAL (PLURAL) _____

TYPE OF FOOD _____

Mrs. Potato Head: Now, my _____, did you pack everything?
SILLY WORD

Mr. Potato _____: I think so, dear, but do I really need all of
PART OF THE BODY

these _____?
PLURAL NOUN

Mrs. Potato Head: _____, of course you do! It's _____
EXCLAMATION _ADJECTIVE_

for a toy to go out unprepared. I packed an extra pair of shoes,

some _____ for if you get hungry, and your angry
TYPE OF FOOD (PLURAL)

_____—just in case!
PART OF THE BODY (PLURAL)

Mr. Potato Head: Easy there! How many _____ can fit
PLURAL NOUN

into one potato?

Mrs. Potato Head: I'll also pack you a golf ball, in case you feel like

_____. And here's a plastic _____, and some
VERB ENDING IN "ING" _NOUN_

extra _____! Ooh, don't forget to pack some monkey
PART OF THE BODY (PLURAL)

chow, too!

Mr. Potato Head: What would I need *that* for?

Mrs. Potato Head: For the _____, of course!
ANIMAL (PLURAL)

Mr. Potato Head: Sheesh. I didn't sign up to be a loaded _____.
TYPE OF FOOD

MAD LIBS® is fun to play with friends, but you can also play it by yourself! To begin with, DO NOT look at the story on the page below. Fill in the blanks on this page with the words called for. Then, using the words you have selected, fill in the blank spaces in the story.

Now you've created your own hilarious MAD LIBS® game!

BO PEEP TALKS SHEEP

ADJECTIVE _____

NOUN _____

NOUN _____

NUMBER _____

VERB _____

PLURAL NOUN _____

VERB _____

ADJECTIVE _____

VERB ENDING IN "ING" _____

VERB _____

VERB _____

ADJECTIVE _____

ADJECTIVE _____

ADJECTIVE _____

PART OF THE BODY _____

NOUN _____

MAD LIBS®

BO PEEP TALKS SHEEP

I may look sweet and _____ , but being a shepherd is no easy
                        ADJECTIVE

_____ . Each morning I wake up at the crack of _____
    NOUN   NOUN

to tend to my flock. Usually, two or _____ sheep are missing,
                                         NUMBER

so I _____ all over the place to find them. Next, I clean their
        VERB

_____ , _____ their hooves, and get them
    PLURAL NOUN   VERB

ready for the day. And don't get me started on the _____
                                                        ADJECTIVE

fighting! Sheep are constantly biting and _____ at
                                              VERB ENDING IN "ING"

each other. It's enough to _____ a person crazy. If you
                               VERB

_____ me, I don't get nearly enough credit around here.
    VERB

Herding sheep is _____ work! Thankfully, my _____
                     ADJECTIVE   ADJECTIVE

little sheep are all I need in this world. Sure, they're bratty and

_____ and a pain in the _____ , but we
  ADJECTIVE   PART OF THE BODY

love each other to the _____ and back.
                           NOUN

MAD LIBS® is fun to play with friends, but you can also play it by yourself! To begin with, DO NOT look at the story on the page below. Fill in the blanks on this page with the words called for. Then, using the words you have selected, fill in the blank spaces in the story.

Now you've created your own hilarious MAD LIBS® game!

DEAR JESSIE

ADJECTIVE _____

PLURAL NOUN _____

VERB _____

PERSON IN ROOM _____

PLURAL NOUN _____

ADJECTIVE _____

ADJECTIVE _____

NOUN _____

VERB ENDING IN "ING" _____

ADJECTIVE _____

ADJECTIVE _____

ADJECTIVE _____

PART OF THE BODY (PLURAL) _____

VERB ENDING IN "ING" _____

ANIMAL _____

MAD LIBS

DEAR JESSIE

Dear Jessie,

Hello! _____ day today, isn't it? Sorry for scribbling this on
　　　　ADJECTIVE

the back of one of Bonnie's _____—it's not ideal, but this
　　　　　　　　　　　　　PLURAL NOUN

is the best I can _____. Ever since we broke out of Sunnyside
　　　　　　　　VERB

Daycare and became _____'s toys, I've had a few
　　　　　　　　　　PERSON IN ROOM

_____ for you. First of all, did I do anything _____
PLURAL NOUN　　　　　　　　　　　　　　　　　　　　　　ADJECTIVE

while I was in my demo or _____ mode? I still can't remember
　　　　　　　　　　　　ADJECTIVE

a/an _____, and sometimes I feel like the others are
　　　NOUN

_____ at an inside joke that I don't know about! Not
VERB ENDING IN "ING"

that I'd be _____ if you laughed; I just want to make sure I
　　　　　ADJECTIVE

didn't do anything _____! Secondly, do you know anything
　　　　　　　　ADJECTIVE

about my _____ dancing? Every time I hear salsa music, my
　　　　ADJECTIVE

_____ just won't quit! I hope you don't mind
PART OF THE BODY (PLURAL)

_____ with me—space rangers and beautiful
VERB ENDING IN "ING"

_____-girls make good dance partners, I guess!
　　ANIMAL

Signed,

Buzz (Lightyear)

MAD LIBS® is fun to play with friends, but you can also play it by yourself! To begin with, DO NOT look at the story on the page below. Fill in the blanks on this page with the words called for. Then, using the words you have selected, fill in the blank spaces in the story.

Now you've created your own hilarious MAD LIBS® game!

GAME NIGHT

CELEBRITY _____

VERB _____

EXCLAMATION _____

NOUN _____

PLURAL NOUN _____

ADJECTIVE _____

ADJECTIVE _____

SAME CELEBRITY _____

NUMBER _____

PLURAL NOUN _____

VERB _____

VERB _____

PART OF THE BODY (PLURAL) _____

ADVERB _____

PART OF THE BODY _____

MAD LIBS®

GAME NIGHT

Trixie: Psst, Rex! Did you hear about the new _____-themed
CELEBRITY

video game? I can download it on the computer right now, and we can

_____!
VERB

Rex: _____, I don't know, Trixie. What if Bonnie wakes up?
EXCLAMATION

Trixie: No worries! Once Mom reads Bonnie a bedtime _____,
NOUN

not even a horde of _____ could wake her up. Come on,
PLURAL NOUN

it'll be _____! The game finally loaded and it looks so
ADJECTIVE

_____!
ADJECTIVE

Rex: Can I play as _____?
SAME CELEBRITY

Trixie: Of course! Ready to start level _____?
NUMBER

Rex: Wait, I don't know which _____ to press! Is there a
PLURAL NOUN

manual?

Trixie: Nope, you gotta _____ as you go—ready, set, _____!
VERB   VERB

Rex: Oh no, my _____ are too short to reach the
PART OF THE BODY (PLURAL)

B button!

Trixie: Oh well! You better think of something else _____,
ADVERB

Rex, because I am kicking your _____!
PART OF THE BODY

MAD LIBS® is fun to play with friends, but you can also play it by yourself! To begin with, DO NOT look at the story on the page below. Fill in the blanks on this page with the words called for. Then, using the words you have selected, fill in the blank spaces in the story.

Now you've created your own hilarious MAD LIBS® game!

YOU'VE GOT A FRIEND IN ME

PLURAL NOUN _____

NOUN _____

NOUN _____

A PLACE _____

PLURAL NOUN _____

NOUN _____

NOUN _____

A PLACE _____

ADJECTIVE _____

PLURAL NOUN _____

NOUN _____

NOUN _____

A PLACE _____

MAD LIBS®

YOU'VE GOT A FRIEND IN ME

Howdy, partner! If you've ever wondered what it means to be a good

toy, have I got some _____ for you:

_____PLURAL NOUN

- Never give up on your _____. When I was Andy's toy, I

_____NOUN

  always chose to be there for him. Once he passed me on to Bonnie,

  I promised the same _____ to her.

_____NOUN

- Playtime is great, but it's not the most important thing in (the)

  _____. Even as your kid grows older, you'll always have

_____A PLACE

  your fellow _____ to keep you company. And if your

_____PLURAL NOUN

  _____ realizes he or she needs you, you'll be right there!

____NOUN

  Which reminds me . . .

- Don't just be a/an _____ to your kid—be a friend to the

_____NOUN

  other toys in (the) _____, too! Buzz and I had a/an

_____A PLACE

  _____ start to our friendship, but now we're the best of

__ADJECTIVE

  _____.

__PLURAL NOUN

Being a/an _____ means so much more than being a piece of

_____NOUN

plastic. It means being a part of a kid's _____ . . . I wouldn't

_____NOUN

trade it for anything in (the) _____!

_____A PLACE

Download Mad Libs today!

Join the millions of Mad Libs fans
creating wacky and wonderful
stories on our apps!